better together*

*This book is best read together, grownup and kid.

a kids
book
about ™

a kids book about™ belonging

by **Kevin Carroll**
Bestselling Author of
Rules of the Red Rubber Ball

a kids book about™

Library of Congress Cataloging-in-Publication Data is available.

This book represents my personal experience and thus is not intended to be representative of every form or example of belonging.

A Kids Book About Belonging is exclusively available online on the a kids book about website.

To share your stories, ask questions, or inquire about bulk purchases (schools, libraries, and non-profits), please use the following email address:

hello@akidsbookabout.com

www.akidsbookabout.com

ISBN: 978-1-951253-03-5

Printed in the USA

Dedicated to the NextGEN of leaders, makers, DOers & dreamers!

Intro

What does it mean to belong? It's difficult to come up with a simple answer, but each of us (kid and grownup) is hoping every day to belong somewhere.

While belonging can be tough to describe, we all know the benefits. Belonging to a community or others improves your health, happiness, and motivation. When you belong, you realize you are not alone. Having a connection to others helps you understand that all of us can have good times, but struggle, too.

There is comfort in knowing we ALL have this in common. To build community, a sense of belonging, and be comfortable in our own skin is a lifelong endeavor. This book wants to help on the journey. Your journey! Because belonging starts with YOU!

Hey you.

Yes **YOU**,
the one reading this book.

Have you ever felt like you don't **belong**?

Like you don't fit in or that other people don't get you?

Well, this is a kids book about **belonging**.

I'm going to tell you what it means to **belong**.

And what it feels like when you don't.

Ok, so this is you.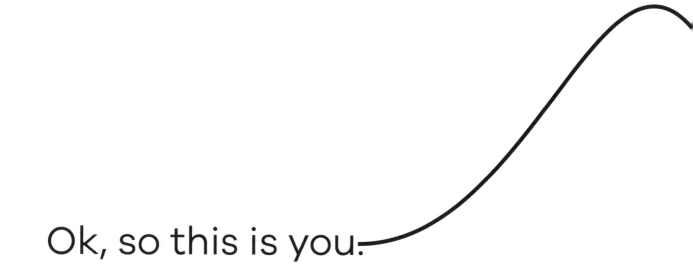

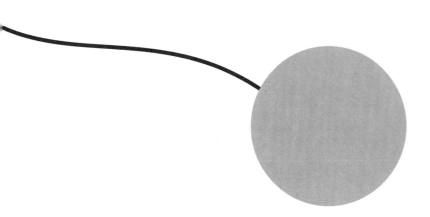

I know, it's just a circle and probably doesn't look like you at all. Just go with me here.

You probably **belong** somewhere right?

A place or group
or activity...

where you feel "at home?"

Like a...

school

team

family

neighborhood

playground

band

or just planet earth.

But, what does it actually mean to **belong**?!

Belonging is when you are a part of something.

When you feel included.

It also means you feel...

SAFE

Like when you're asleep
in bed...

or when you're eating your favorite food.

Belonging is quite simply

cool, good, and wonderful!

But sometimes it feels like you don't **belong**.

Like others don't want you around.

Like

you

want

to

be

anywhere

else.

Like you're not safe.

Like you can't be you.

Have you ever felt like that?

It's not cool or good
or wonderful.

Right?!

It can feel...

Lonely
Painful
Unsafe
Scary
and Sad.

Sometimes it looks like not getting picked to play on the team.

And sometimes it's getting left out.

Other times,
you're invited...

but you
don't feel comfortable.

You might even think that you need to pretend you're somebody you're not, just to **belong**.

Or that you need to wear a mask to fit in.

That way, maybe you'll **belong**...

Right?

Honestly,
that will just make
things worse.

Trust me.

Because...

Belonging is...

CONNECTION

SUPPORT

COMFORT

AND SAFETY

So what should you

(YES YOU!)

do when you
feel like you don't
belong?

I'm glad you asked.

Remember...

that you must **belong** to yourself first.

I know, I know you're wondering what in the world that means?

It means you must...

Love yourself

Accept yourself

Like yourself

Appreciate yourself

Care for yourself

And support yourself

Because

BELO

IGING
starts with you!

When you **belong** to yourself, just as you are, with no faking or pretending....

You'll always **belong**,
no matter where you are.

It makes it ok when you don't fit in, because you know that you don't have to.

And when you do fit,
you know it's because
you're being **YOU**!

So first...

belong to yourself.

And second...

find those
people, places, and groups
that you can **belong** to,
just by being you.

That's it!

Outro

Belonging is so essential to our lives. When you don't have a sense of belonging anywhere, it can feel like living in a world without oxygen.

Grownup, this is your chance to share a story about when you felt like you didn't belong and what you did when that happened. Invite them in, and they may just do the same with you.

This is a wonderful opportunity to start a conversation and not let it end with this book. If you're willing to be honest and transparent and a bit vulnerable, the result will be informative, enlightening, and uplifting conversations. Kids are ready and willing to learn about tough things, as long as the grownups in their lives are courageous and willing to talk about them. GameON!